"*When One World Ends, Another Begins* is an introspective tapestry of poetry that is as profound as it is touching. Sweet, melancholy, and heartfelt, this collection touches the soul while its spell lingers long after the final poem."

-Pedro Iniguez, author of *Mexicans on the Moon: Speculative Poetry from a Possible Future*

"Sharp. Profound. A heart wrenching tribute to poetry itself and how it lives within the body before it moves down the page. It's a poet's cycle of drowning under the weight of the world, followed by desperate gasps of stardust that flood the veins with hope. Luscombe's poetry will carve a place to live among your bones."

-R.C. Lloyd, author of *Chronic Defiance*

"The first half of this book's initials spell out WOW, which pretty much describes my reaction to this stunning little poetry collection. Nathaniel Luscombe probes the depths of space and humanity alike through poems that are both gentle and powerful, with rich metaphors and relatable themes. This collection is sure to touch hearts, stir minds, and delight the souls of poets-at-heart."

-Amelia E Clawford, author in *Unleash the Cosmos*

"Nathaniel Luscombe inspires hope and the space to be real through crisp and compelling verse. In artistic style, he presents the human condition of moving from one chapter of life to another by peeling open old wounds, studying them, and carefully healing them. He paints a stunning picture of what it means to be alive and finding hope despite pain, all while traversing a beautiful, untamed, and sometimes unkind universe."

-Michaela Bush, author of *Everything I Became*

"This is a poetry collection fit for everyone. It holds themes of time and love, sorrow and existentialism, peace and life and death. It is a collection about the stars, the universe, and ultimately, oneself. It is best described as a grouping of love letters to the human condition. Reading this is akin to an act of self care."

-Erelah Emerson, author of *Erratic and Unnecessary*

"Utterly evocative and piercingly beautiful, Luscombe has proved himself to be a poet to watch with his newest collection, When One World Ends, Another Begins. His poetic skill is one to be envied. You'll be highlighting the whole way through this collection, I know I was."

-Stephanie Dunham, author of *Everything is Okay*

WHEN ONE WORLD ENDS, ANOTHER BEGINS

POEMS

NATHANIEL LUSCOMBE

Also by Nathaniel Luscombe

Moon Soul

The Planets We Become

Human Scars on Planet Skin

Anthologies:

Unleash the Cosmos

Aphotic Love

I Love You Unconventionally

A Sky of Tragic Moons

Also from Dragon Heart Press

Tending Clay; Unearthing Stars by MJ Anthony

When

One

World

Ends

p
o
e
t
r
y

Another

Begins

Nathaniel Luscombe

To Effie, Micah, Jenni, and Beca.
You've helped me move into a new
beginning.
-N.L.

Table of Contents

First Steps

this is a beginning
the previous end still in sight
we've turned to meet
whatever comes next
for now the ground is firm
though that doesn't last long
in this ever-tilting life

with a silent prayer
(perhaps plea is better)
we take our first steps
into the suffocating dark

a beginning
we've been here before
circled the sun enough
to know that every beginning
is just the start of
the end

Vicious Cycles

each day ends as it begins
a pile of faded memories
shoved into a forgotten drawer
a fresh layer of pain(t)
drying on the walls
for a day is a day is a day
and we're all just surviving
moving from one to the next
weary in repetition
washed out in this cycle
we've placed ourselves in
living and loving and
leaving and learning
again and again and
(you guessed it)
again

Bleeding

I read someone else's words
And suddenly I'm bleeding
All over the floor
I've picked at a scab
Opened a wound I forgot I had
Remembered just how confusing
My insides really are
I spend so much time hiding
From others, from myself
Wandering the maze of my body
Lost, always lost
With no map to guide me home

Home, as if I'm not already here
As if these bones haven't housed me
For an exciting twenty one years
Yet I still don't understand myself
Or the ways I become small
When the world turns on me

I'm always running and expanding
Like some sort of rabid universe
The edges are never within reach
The panic is always blaring
The loneliness is always pulsing

And my footprints are scars
Warning me not to turn back

Saturn's Screams

Carve out the sound of my voice.
Make a notch for each tone, each word,
each breath that escapes my lungs.

>My existence has been summed up
>in words I can't say out loud.
>I rest in the vacuum of space.

>>You'll spot me in a trail of stardust.
>>There's but inches of glass between us,
>>yet we're nowhere near each other.

>You don't hear what I hear.
>The universe hums in my veins.
>I'm an atom in a nebulous body.

Sometimes I feel more than I know.
When I can't open my mouth,
I lose myself in Saturn's screams.

I Have Given Much, But Taken Little

Why is it that pain feels alive
and sorrow burrows deep
but joy is surface level
and vanishes in the smallest shadows?

Why is it that to cry is to give
to be silent is to wither
and to speak is to take
when there is no one to take from?

Falling / Flying

Somehow I wandered into adulthood
without knowing what it meant
to leave the younger years behind.
I didn't know I'd be pushing myself every day,
climbing higher and higher,
each time having further to fall.
How long do I have to fall
before falling is considered flying?
To perpetually fall is to always be airborne
and what is flying if not
a constant search for ground?
One day I will find my footing.
I will fall, though I hope it will be
more of a landing,
and the place I end up in will feel like home.
Until then, I'll keep falling / flying / finding myself.

You Are A Door

you stand before an opportunity
and realize the door is locked
and the door is yourself
and you will never get through
no matter how hard you push

Have You Forgotten?

Have you forgotten what it is to be alive? Cherish each day. Remember that life is never guaranteed and the fact that you even opened your eyes this morning is a gift. You're still in this race, and while you've left some people behind, they would want you to make it further than they did.

Have you forgotten that people love you? Linger in their hugs, their warm words, their encouragement. Use their support as crutches to keep you standing. When you feel the holes within you growing bigger, allow them to be filled. Remember it is not weak to speak, not weak to need, not weak to seek help.

Have you forgotten what it is to enjoy beauty? Stand outside your door and take a breath. Look at the flowers, the grass. Hear the birds sing. Watch as the rain dances across your windows, listen to the way the wind howls as it gives chase. Lose yourself in a thunderstorm. Sit in the dark with a good song. Read a book and follow its words to a world unknown. It's up to you to find beauty. Once you do, don't let it go.

Orbital Bones

I've seen eyes that carry time
past present future
stretched from pupil to orbit

Orbit
As if the eye is a planet
trapped in an orbit of bone

E
N
D
L
E
S
S
L
Y

S
P
I
N
N
I
N
G

There is much to take in
during our stay on this planet,

yet

where we go we have already been
what we see we have already seen

somewhere   sometime
beyond our memory.

and what is this beauty

who is that
bleeding between cracked mirrors
and what is that torment
coming from within

my eyes pick up on beauty
in everything but myself

i am not tied to my body
and i sometimes forget it exists
because who i am inside
does not feel like
this

there must be something
i don't see
and perhaps no one sees it
for if these words come from my heart
i know there's beauty in me
that i'm still learning to care for

Silent Skin, Screaming Bones

I was raised to fill this silent skin
so I sought refuge between
my screaming bones

I drowned beneath my own weight
full of words I could not say
I took to carving them
into the fabric of my being
scared I'd forget myself
if I was quiet for too long

There were stages of anger
where everything felt like too much
but I learned to hold it all in

At least I thought I did

Words became my bloodletting
I've been bleeding now for years

Syzygy

This
alignment
in threes.

The beauty of
Earth
Moon
Sun

casting their shadows
to become glowing rings
in the Milky Way

The surety of
Faith
Hope
Love

forming a foundation that holds
while the universe collapses
and the light turns to dark

Even God comes in three
and perhaps that is the pattern
that shaped us all

Mirroring the Universe

I run across the glassy ocean
and lose myself in the reflection of the stars
there's no escape from the mirror of the universe
no escape from what I see within
perception is a beast with sharp teeth
and peace has too heavy a price
if only I could break the tension
and dive away from the starry eyes

April 8th, 2024

Living is more than existing.
It's lining up by the side of the road
because the universe is aligning
and we want to stand in its shadow.

It's staring in awe at the totality
and feeling lost and found
in the beauty of it all.

It's forgetting, just for a minute,
the weight of the burdens
that tie us to this Earth.

Escaping Orbit

I can't seem to get a good grip.
My fingers slip between stars,
shoulders aching as I try to move.
A trail of stardust behind me,
the promise of light before me.
There is no end to this circular universe,
stories repeated over and over,
the same pain, the same hopelessness.
Breaking this orbit is hard.
The gravity of doubt,
of guilt, of fear.
The weight of living.
It holds me back,
it fuels me forward,
always searching for the next handhold

The Whole of Our Existence

I would like to fall back
into the arms of the one
who wove tapestries from stardust
and twisted light into galaxies

I want to feel the security
of one who is sure
that the whole of their existence
fits safely into the palm of someone else

I want to read between the stars
and find the living story
that speaks of hope and love
to those who feel lost

Too often I lay beneath ceilings
and try to find meaning
in the stars I've hung myself

I feel the closeness of the walls
the pressure of the ceiling
the weight of the world

I am begging to be freed
from a cage I've built myself

NATHANIEL LUSCOMBE

Dust, You Say?

You say we are dust,
trodden underfoot,
a well-worn path
of weary souls
and tired bodies.

I say we are stardust,
formed from mysteries,
a map of what has been
and what is to come

Do not be reduced
to common dust
when you have thick roots
in an endless universe.

Afar

I write about the universe too much
for someone who has never left Earth.
What do I know of moons, stars,
or the winding arms of a galaxy?
Who am I to speak of their beauty?
Me, who has never seen them
without an atmospheric lens
to dim their heavenly glow.

I have one thing to my name:

Wonder

This is what I hold.
I have soaked in it,
dyed my bones with it,
and now my words
drip
with
it.

I cannot create
without acknowledging the beauty
that fills the space around me.
I hold tight to any art,

30

natural or created,
because it is a reflection
of a universe afar.

Wellness

Being alive and being well
are not the same thing.
We are a land of living dead.
Our bodies have been compressed
until we no longer feel at home.
We strain against our skin
and clamber across our bones
but there is no escape.

skinned and peeled

love is a peeling, aching thing
revealing the writhing mess
we are beneath this skin

our only skin

the skin we are granted
to bear from birth to death
bear as a burden, bear as a gift
of which we feel undeserving

and love is an eye
from which there is no escape

in its gaze, we feel at peace
with the occasional taste of fear
perhaps the intruding feeling
that we do not deserve this love
do not deserve to feel at peace

do not deserve this skin we're in
or the way time has cradled us

but to be loved is to be at peace
and it is the most wonderful, frightening,

delicious thing to allow the taste of peace
to linger like a hearty feast

Stone

the freedom of poetry is not for everyone
the lack of form annoys them
the self-awareness scares them
the mirror turns them to stone

Soft Hearts

Warn the soft hearts
that the universe is not kind,
and has, in fact,
conspired against us
to be cold and hard
when we just need a place to rest

Perhaps this is what life is:
endless searching,
bitter acceptance,
a sort of tired hope.

In between:
moments of peace,
where love shines through,
where hope is tangible
and wraps its arms around us.

Occasionally:
feeling small,
looking at the stars,
thinking about the finite nature of life,
the fear of open space,
the beating heart that holds it all together.

Finally:
realizing we are soft on our own,
not because of our surroundings,
and we can continue so
even when the universe has blades
and we have blankets.

A Slow Apocalypse

The world is burning,
or perhaps it always was
and we only now learned to see,
to fear, to question, to work
to save this global home.

We have set our own fires,
that much is clear,
and while the world would always die
perhaps we've shaved off too many years.

This world is all we are,
past, present, and ~~future~~.
when it surrenders to flames,
we surrender with it,
layers of history put to rest.

Heatwave

I am reduced to nothing
in the midst of a heatwave.
No thoughts, no motivation,
just the mundane pushing on,
the daily struggle of living.

It's exhausting, fearing the future
but running from the past.
I want to continue forward
into a world of heatwaves,
wars, uncertainties,
but also victories, dreams,
and independence.

I cling to hope
even when it shakes me off.

Slice of Life

waking beneath a flaming sky
of pink clouds chasing orange hues
while the sun struggles to rise

drinking up the morning
in all its unwavering glory

lost between the birdsong
lost in general
for we cannot be found
if we never wander off
the well-trodden path

following the babbling rivers
into the wilderness of living

all of us stragglers

all of us finally alive

through the ice

thinking about how
we used to skate on little ponds
between coarse grass
and muskrat homes

snow in our hot chocolate
sitting on little logs
the cows watching from afar

and now the winters barely stay
and our feet break right through
the ice we once glided across

Oh

Golden hour:
when the sun drapes itself
across our tired land
and the heat quiets
to give us rest.

Oh, sun
Oh, warmth
Oh, yellow

I catch reflections of the day
across white walls.
Like paint, except it does not dry.
A moving mural,
scattering,
playing the memories back
until the light fades.

Oh, moon
Oh, rest
Oh, black

Beneath the twinkling skies,
I lay with eyes wide open.
There is a story to be told,

42

where constellations move
to their unheard choir
and the universe unfurls
to keep up with this song

Oh, stars
Oh, wind
Oh, life

Still Waters

I stand in a rushing flood
that just can't let me go
an unstoppable deluge
carving canyons in my soul
when all I seek are still waters

May 10th, 2024

You have not lived
until you see a sunset bleed
into the northern lights
The universe reveals itself
amid a dance of colors
Green ripples to red ripples to orange
and the naked eye struggles
but the digital eye captures perfectly
this wild experience on a breezy spring night
It's nights like this that I cling to faith
because this beauty feels bigger
than just sun streaks across a dark sky

a gentle stream of necessary thoughts

captivated at the space between joy and sorrow / the way it can stretch for an eternity / the way it can kiss at any moment / the way we usually hold hands with both, though we do our best to not let the other see / cheating on joy with sorrow and on sorrow with joy / cheating on ourselves / mesmerized by the tear and the way it must be spun and translated before one knows whether it contains joy or sorrow / a happy tear is as salty as a sad tear / both come from the same well / who gave permission for this water to gather within me / who decided we would react with tears to every big moment / speared with the reality that tears are just the beginning of a feeling / crying with sadness is like being swallowed and only having the strength to squeeze out one last gesture / it's a small testament to the storm boiling inside / crying with joy is the unleashing of self / it's a piece of modern art, a simple line that cannot fully bear the width of what's happening inside / happiness often leads to sadness because there is sadness in knowing that happiness ends / everything ends / weighed with the knowledge that ending is part of starting / why does my mind always drift to the sad things / my thoughts are rocks around my feet / the very act of existing is an ocean of uncertainty / to bring these thoughts back around, to create a circle, i must take comfort in water / i have always loved how water runs in a cycle / each raindrop is a memory / each storm is a history / we stand in the rain and are touched by the same drop that ran from adam's eyes as he was banished from the garden of eden / we cup our hands and hold the same rain that washed over a dinosaur / in a smaller sense, we connect to the water that has sustained all the life present with us on this small planet / each tear returns to the earth / joy and sorrow united once again

Who Are You to Judge Me?

I have given up too much of myself
to be small in the eyes of strangers.
Me, who stands above a crowd,
who speaks loudly and laughs even louder,
always trying to tame the sound
within my too-big body.

I limit myself through the eyes of people
I hope I'll never meet again.
I feel watched, always watched,
as if the world is an inescapable eye
and I'm dancing across the pupil.
I wish the world would go blind.

Poetry

These words taste of honey
Of blood of rage
Of desperation to be seen
Yet desperation to remain unseen
They try to hide my fear
But these words have always been transparent

Life on a Page

How quickly we skip across time
and how short this space is
between the beginning and the end.
One day we inhale for the first time,
the next we exhale until we are empty,
and between those breaths…
what?
How do we make sense of the inbetween?
With every joy comes a sorrow
and victory is married to loss.
We wrestle with our worth
and in the end we feel worthless.

the universe + a finger

and in one moment
spoken upon fiery breath
all that is
came to be
a second of eternity
became eternity in a second
as the universe spun
around the finger
of its creator

Holding Time's Hand

drowning in memories

                                  clutching the future

               ignoring the present
                 time slipping

always slipping

                          a wet slippery thing

                time is

          i have not learned to hold it
              nor cage it
           nor use it for myself

            centuries ahead
         when i'm buried in dust
         time will still move on
       unhindered by base desire
       by anger or hunger or fear
        marching ever on beyond
       suns exploding and stars

             oh stars

bleeding out their light
as a coldness creeps
through the black void

i must take time's hand
where i stand
and hold fast to its present form

All of Us Parallel

time is but an orchestra
past present future
the three tender strings
that cut through a universe
beyond our comprehension

no fingers could coax them
to make a sound so sweet
it would break our pain

we are all of us parallel
playing out our roles
in a never ending cycle
birthing bleeding dying
again and again and again

Languages of Hurt

We miss the sorrow
in each others eyes
because we don't know how to hurt
in the same language.

Remember to Cry

When all is said and done,
remember to cry.
Those who do not cry
become full of their sorrow
until it rusts them out
in desperation to escape

Widen the cracks,
free the sea,
remember to cry.

another life

I yearn for the freedom of another life
another universe
where I don't hold myself back
don't live in constant fear
instead learning to let go
never losing myself
in the could-have-beens
never turning to a pillar of salt
with my eyes locked
on the fires of the past

frantic scrawlings of one who will be forgotten

we fit ourselves between the bones
we've been given
and pray they don't hurt

we are told to be content
that we are not meant for more
we get what we get
no questions asked
and after it all
we end as we started

no record of the life we lived

yet is this not why we're alive?
is this not why we're ambitious?
to become someone beyond
the person we were at birth?

cutting ourselves into sentences
fitting those sentences to pages
binding ourselves wholly
into the things we create

hungering, but not too much
asking, but not expecting
breaking our bones as we go

The Burst

In the wake of a sentence
Lies the form of its writer
Each word weighed carefully
Balancing the scales of perception

Then come the consumers
Devouring these words
Relishing the burst between their teeth
As they tear the sentences apart
And feed on their bleeding insides

I should sever myself from these words
Save myself the blood, the pain
The uncomfortableness of it all
But what good would it be to consume
A word without any life in it?

My Body is Not Me (except it is)

I've come to accept myself
bound between the bones
of a body I don't like

there is fear in every layer
fear of myself, fear of the world
fear of people seeing me
fear of people not seeing me

I only love my eyes
for the way they see the world
limitless, beautiful,
unlike me.

A Place to Feel at Home

I hope you can find yourself here,
hiding behind my words.
Maybe I can coax you out,
offer you some comfort,
help you feel welcomed.
We'll sit here, you and I,
while you read and I write.
Work through the words at your own pace,
stay on the pages that feel like home.
If you come across a mirror,
I promise not to tell you what I see.
Just know that I'm a home
and I have room for many.

Change

I feel myself changing
for better or worse
because there's a bitterness
I didn't have a year ago
but also some form of peace

Perhaps I found my voice
and it made me angry
or I found it in anger
or anger is my voice
but I'm not an angry person

At least I wasn't
but I'm still learning about
this new person I've become
the one who speaks up a little more
and listens a little less

I've come to accept the price of speaking:
a rapidly beating heart
an out-of-tune song in my veins
and a small sense of self
growing bigger with each word

Word Vomit

sometimes i worry about the words i write
and what they say about me
i am the mind that carried these words
before they were birthed into existence
i have created whole worlds in my head
built up characters and fabricated problems
(not all these problems are fictional)
i wonder if people see the secrets
i've left in all the white space
follow the trail i've scattered for those
who care to follow to the end (am i the end?)
i feel this weight as i grow bolder in my words
because i'm writing what i feel
(should i hold myself back?)
and what i feel won't please everyone

sometimes i wish my writing was a secret
under some other name so i didn't have to
carry these words with me in 'real life'
(how easily we hide who we are in fear)

Time Pivots

I don't fear aging on this end of the spectrum
where age is a lovely thing, bringing freedom
and an abundance of new experiences.
But when does time pivot?
When do I reach the middle
where I realize that what goes up must stay up?
Going up, up, up
until my body can no longer contain itself
and I begin breaking down in terrifying ways.
I'll wear my age on my skin,
feel its weight on my bones,
and one day I'll be forgotten.

Bury Me Beneath My Words

Bury me beneath my words
so they may hold me down.
I want to carry them with me
when I cross into the end
The words I **wrote**
The words I **loved**
The words I **hid**
Death is not a time for hiding.
It's a time for all to be made clear,
and I have always spoken best in writing.
Do not separate me from my words,
I beg you, but lay them down with me
so I may be remembered,
so I may remember.

some say prayers, others write poems

our world is not one of biblical proportions
where miracles lay around every corner
and god reveals himself to veiled faces

it is one of blind faith
inner assurance
silent hope

do angels linger among us?
or has heaven turned its back
on this ever-crumbling world?

we have more questions than answers
it seems
and who can we ask?

who has spoken to god?

am i speaking to god
through my irregular poetry
taken straight from the heart?

it's easier to write these poems
than it is to pray

because i know where these poems go
but i can't track a prayer

maybe prayers never leave
maybe they stay within us
where god lives
warming the temple
we've forgotten to use

and angels don't have to linger
because they wrapped their wings
around our tender souls

and heaven hasn't turned its back
because we live in its shattered reflection
while walking toward its glorious reality

Questions

Never be ashamed of asking questions.
One who asks is always seeking,
always looking for more,
always learning,
always open to being wrong.

One who shames a questioner is a fool.
They are wise by their own discretion,
trapped in a fishbowl of reasoning.
When the fishbowl breaks
and the water pours out,
they are left gasping for air,
unable to breathe
in a world not built for them.

living in motion

i am
a soul living
in a body spinning
on a planet hurtling
through the endless universe

wracked with motion sickness
all of me moving at once
my heart beating and
my veins pumping and
my mind contemplating
the depths of the stars

Lose Yourself

Lose yourself
in a little song
you leave on repeat.

Find yourself
in a little painting
you see in a gallery.

Become this art.
Let it feed you.
For without art,
who are you?

Let it show you
the inner workings
of another mind.

Let it assure you
that you're okay,
you who feels so anxious.

Remember that you
only know your body,
your thoughts, your fears,
but through art you can know
more than you've ever known before.

Oceans & Stars

oceans are meant
to mirror the stars
for those who haven't learned
to look up

Icarus Drowning

in the end
that's all he was

a cloud of feathers

falling
amid cries
from a desperate
father who couldn't
save his own
son

s p i n n i n g

the world tilting around him
hungry waves ready to devour
the young spirit of icarus

and that's where it ends

we don't talk about him drowning
because he wanted to hold the sun

Affinity for the Unspoken Words

When did I learn to hear
between the lines of life,
picking up on the unspoken words
that bear more weight
than my lips can bear?

To speak a word
is to bring it into existence.
It creates a physical burden
that notches hearts
lingering for years to come.

We are but dams for these words
and we feel them every day,
the way they push for freedom,
the cracks they make between our pores.
We bite tongues and clench teeth
and fill with words until we die.

Box

these walls are set in the stars
drawn in a constellation
that holds me in
cold, endless arms
wrapped around my neck

this is the box I stay in
if I want to feel loved

this is the box I stay in
if I want my universe in one piece

I feel the cracks sometimes
have cut myself on them
blood mixing with tears

These walls have contained my fears
and I've drowned in them
become them

Wholly
Unspeakably

Curdled Words

I swallow words like milk gone bad
Curdled lumps catching in a thirsty throat
They always come back up
My soul unable to digest the hurt
(Because hurt goes down a different throat
Not to the stomach, but to the soul
Where it festers)
I weaponize my pain internally
A knife buried in my gut
Do I swallow words or do they swallow me?

Tinnitus

Even away from it all
I carry music with me
as a ringing in my ears
(at times gentle, at times a waterfall
of overwhelming stimulation)

If only I could inject it into my veins
and experience that all-encompassing sound
without the art also becoming a burden

Google told me tinnitus also stems from anxiety
It makes sense, I suppose,
as I always have a song on my lips
and an ache in my heart

Unravel the Self

I lose myself
to the slippery confines of my mind
where memories wash on the shore
of cerebral matter

I've been here before

D
R
O
W
N
I
N
G

I've found parts of myself
that scare me

Gasping for air between
all I've become

A hollow reflection dancing
upon waves of uncertainty

I am here/I am he/I am
I have yet to unravel who I am

78

Vulnerability

Words come harder than they should
perhaps we're still finding
the voice that has been waiting
but more likely we're scared
and we don't want to speak
because speaking is a window
and we haven't yet cleaned
the messy rooms of our soul

Preparing for the Fall

I can't seem to understand
pride as a bad thing
because I have to dig so deep
into the inner parts of myself
before I find pride
for any of the things I've done

I've climbed over
emotional mountain ranges
just to get where I am
yet I'm emotionally cold
to all the good I've done
I can only see
the failure along the way

It hurts to know I can't
acknowledge myself

If I can't
then who?

Who is going to remind me
that each day of life
is a priceless opportunity

and everything I do
is worth the failure?

I will find a piece of pride
somewhere in this body
and cherish it before the fall

Overgrown

all I wanted was for the moss
to tenderly make its way across my skin
followed by the spreading fungi
and an ecosystem of bugs
creating life in death
my bones becoming homes
my mind finally empty
the earth taking back what it wants

instead the weeds crept in
and corrupted this fading home
the well-fanged thistles
and deeply rooted rot
chased away any sort of life

now
all around is deathly still
and I am dead still

Mindful

Mindful
as in full of my mind and
wholly consumed by my thoughts
constantly outrunning myself
only to turn around
because this is where I feel safest

To Be Human is to Take Up Space

You have worn yourself out
trying not to take up space
I see the way you hug
your sides as if your arms
are constantly in the way

I want you to exist
freely, warmly, happily,
taking up the space you
earn just by being alive

even the dead take up space
and why should you care
about the space you need now
when you'll eventually die
and be stuck in a box?

Swing your arms out
(carefully, thoughtfully)
and revel in the fact
that you control the
size of the box you
place yourself in

Exit Wound

my mouth is an exit wound
spilling blood from the
hurt pooling inside.
without these poems,
I would not understand
how much I burn beneath
this paper-thin skin.
the tender heart
wants what it wants
but it has never known
how to put its needs
into words.
I write what I know
not understanding why
I'm always falling apart.
These words are a knife
cutting through bone,
opening my chest cavity,
revealing innards
of an emotional sort.
my mouth is an exit wound.
it's hurting and healing
and I'm going to be okay.

When One World Ends

as little things add up
they feel like the end
they're inescapable
uncertainty leading to rot
stress bringing on heart pains
still I grow older
and it's harder to put down roots
the ones I have aren't deep
and the wind takes me in one gust
tossed through the sky
landing in a place I don't know

yet/yet

the world only gets smaller with time
which can be good
but
more often it's not
I'm trapped in a mindscape
where I fall with my thoughts
and rise with my hope

through it all
I've learned that when one world ends
another begins

Another Begins (postlude)

anything can be world-ending/death/sorrow/a
tender blend of both/the loneliness you feel when
walking down an empty sidewalk/the way you
shudder when you realize that everyone you walk
past is alive/the moment a mistake sends your
heart shrieking to your soles/the blank stare at the
clock as time continues moving without your
permission

there will be an end to every world
and a beginning will always follow

this is a beginning

as a thank you for reading this book & purchasing
the paperback, you can download the ebook
version in our store for free!

dragonbonepublishing.gumroad.com

w-qb3oxxl

AUTHOR'S LETTER

I didn't fall in love with poetry until I started writing it. Once I explored it outside of a classroom and tasted the freedom within writing poetry, I couldn't stop.

And now, three years later, I have managed to wrangle together a complete collection.

This collection means a lot to me. It wasn't until I put it together that I realized how thematic my poetry is. In writing these poems, I accidentally stumbled across the puzzle pieces of my mind, and now I feel a little more complete. I understand myself more.

It's scary knowing that anyone can pick up this collection. I cover a lot of topics and they're all so important to me. I want people like me to pick this up and see themselves in it. I want them to realize that it's okay to feel like a stranger in the only home you've ever known. We're all living life for the first time. We don't know what we're doing. There's no in-depth tutorial for how to live. The best we can do is take each day as it comes and try to turn it into something beautiful.

So if you've gotten to the end of this collection and you're feeling a lot of things, let me ground you again.

You are an amazing human being.

Nobody else can be who you are.

You're exactly who you're meant to be at this moment.

You should not be afraid of change. Change doesn't always mean letting go of things. Sometimes it's embracing new things and adding them to the collection of your life.

You are a light to the people who are meant to be in your life.

I say all of that because it's what I need to hear sometimes. I wrote a collection of poetry about things ending and beginning, and how sometimes we need to keep walking into the unknown because that's where the world is waiting for us, and it helped me realize just how excited I should be about living. So much has happened within the last two years. I'm building up my dreams brick by brick and I'm still so young. There's so much time ahead of me (hopefully (sorry that's the scared part of me talking)) and I can't wait to see what else I do in this crazy thing we call life.

Come, join me in this journey. I'm sure there are many amazing destinations ahead of us.

Nathaniel Luscombe,
2024/12/10

ACKNOWLEDGMENTS

Let's start this off with a guessing game.

Who is my best friend, business partner, cover designer, formatter (sometimes), and number one supporter?

If you didn't guess Effie Joe Stock, you're wrong. I have to start off my acknowledgments screaming about how much Effie means to me. Within a year, she has made most of my author dreams come true. I released a book with a GORGEOUS cover, I became the co-head of an incredible company, and I opened up a poetry imprint (that I get to co-run with another bestie?! Shoutout to Micah). I wouldn't have done any of that without the help of Effie. I am so grateful every day that we found each other in the mess that is social media.

Next I have to thank someone who is just as important. Micah. How do I even begin? You are the reason I first started writing poetry. When you announced an anthology way back in 2020, I sat down and wrote my first poem outside of a school assignment because I was desperate to be published. You have been an incredible friend. This is just the beginning of our poetry adventures and I can't wait to see where we end up. I believe we are doing powerful things together.

Jenni and Beca. The people you are. I don't know how I got so lucky to have two mega talented authors and poets also consider me as a friend, but I hit the jackpot and I will be grateful until the day I die. Thank you for the endless support. It truly means the world to me.

The Moon Soul Besties. You supported me through one of the most incredible periods of my life, and you continue to support me in ways I can't even comprehend. Just having a group of people who are passionate about my writing is enough to make me realize I've made it. This is the life I always dreamed of. Thank you for being such a big part of it.

There are so many other people. I can't even begin to list them all. If you know you've had a positive impact on my life, this paragraph is for you. I love you. I'm happy you're part of my life. I can't wait to watch you do incredible things. How many times can I say incredible? I feel like I've said it a LOT.

But these are my acknowledgments and I'm lucky to know a lot of great (incredible) people.

Thank you.

ABOUT THE AUTHOR

Nathaniel Luscombe is an author and publisher from Ontario, Canada. He's known for his existential writing, weird mashups of speculative genres, and making everything cozy (even horror). His most popular work is his science-fantasy novella *Moon Soul*. When he's not writing, he's busy co-running Dragon Bone Publishing and Dragon Heart Press. *When One World Ends, Another Begins* is his debut poetry collection.

If you enjoyed this collection, you might like these other titles!

Tending Clay; Unearthing Stars
by MJ Anthony

Today I am learning // to take anxiety by the hand // and teach this trembling, fragile beast // that we are (and yet will be) // okay.

In their debut collection, MJ Anthony navigates a complicated web of intersecting topics such as complex trauma, neurodiversity, lasting illness, and practicing self-love in a body long-alienated from you. Alongside the reader, the author combs tangles into threads and weaves them into a gentler future, reunifying selves and stories both old and new.

Part hurting, part healing, and wholly original, *Tending Clay; Unearthing Stars* is a love letter to everyone living with a broken body or a troubled mind.

Moon Soul

by Nathaniel Luscombe

"I don't think I can justify it any longer. I'm going to quit my job."

August has never been good with change and isn't sure who she is beyond her job of reading memories in the sand. When she comes to the conclusion that she has to quit her job, she's left with an overwhelming sense of emptiness. What follows is the quiet chaos of a girl regaining control over her life on a small desert moon.

Deciding to take a job in the hanging gardens of the Spire, August discovers more to life as she meets new friends, forms a different connection with her home, and faces an unexpected visitor from her past.

Rich in relatable emotions and experiences, inspiring in message, and written in prose that will hook you from page one, Moon Soul is a science fantasy novella unlike any you've read before. It will leave you feeling seen and understood.

Unleash the Cosmos: A Space Poetry Anthology
edited by Nathaniel Luscombe and Jenni Sauer

Discover a spaceship in your backyard, send your run-on wishes into space, take a bite of space toast, and drink some starlight on tap.

These fifty poems are a love letter to the vast variety of emotions we experience when thinking about the universe. You're invited to find a cozy spot, look up at the stars, take a deep breath, and revel in the wonders, hope, fear, and heartbreak of the endless cosmos.

Perfect for fans of Nathaniel Luscombe, Becky Chambers, and Alex Silvius.